JDM
COLORING BOOK

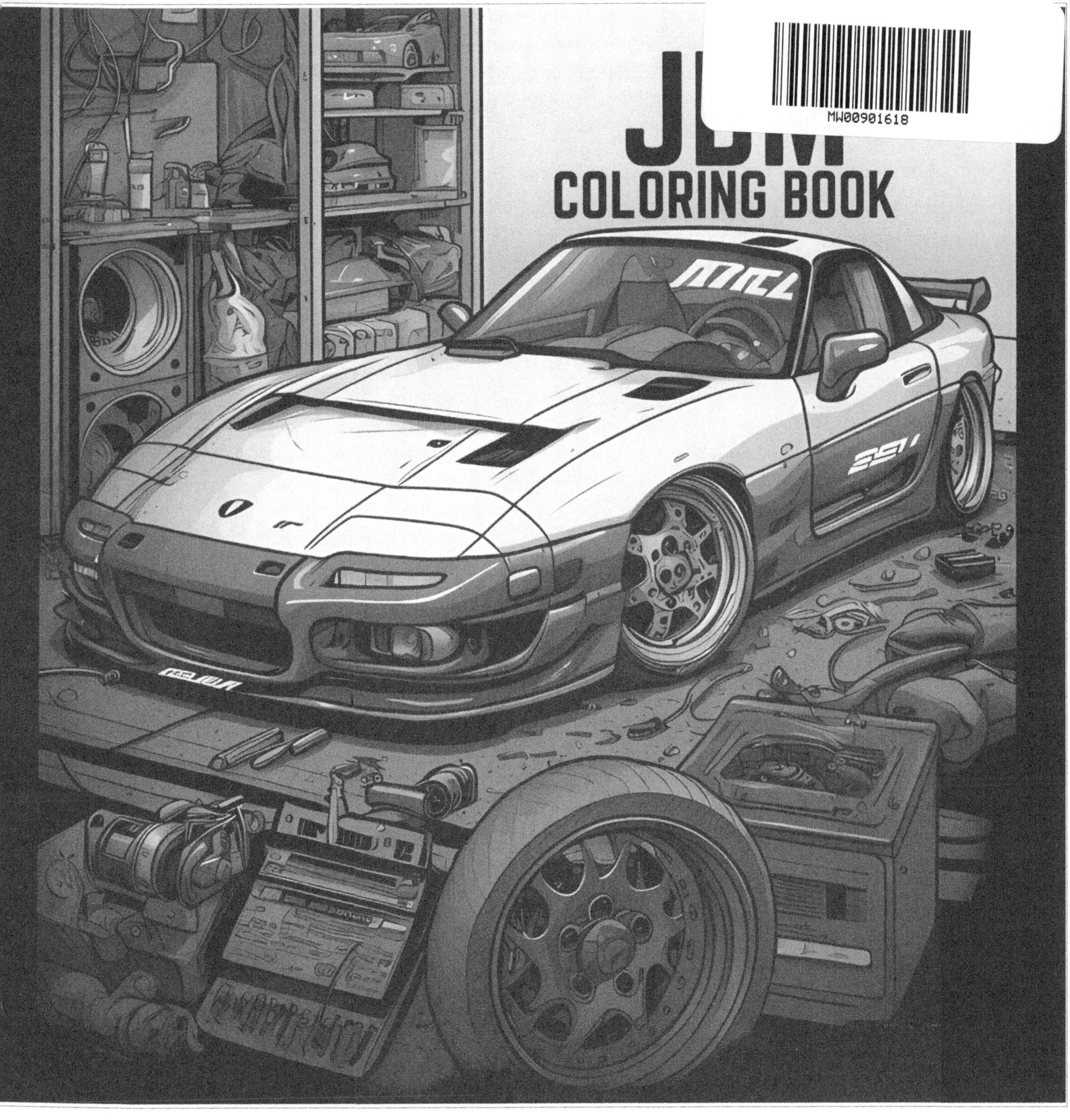

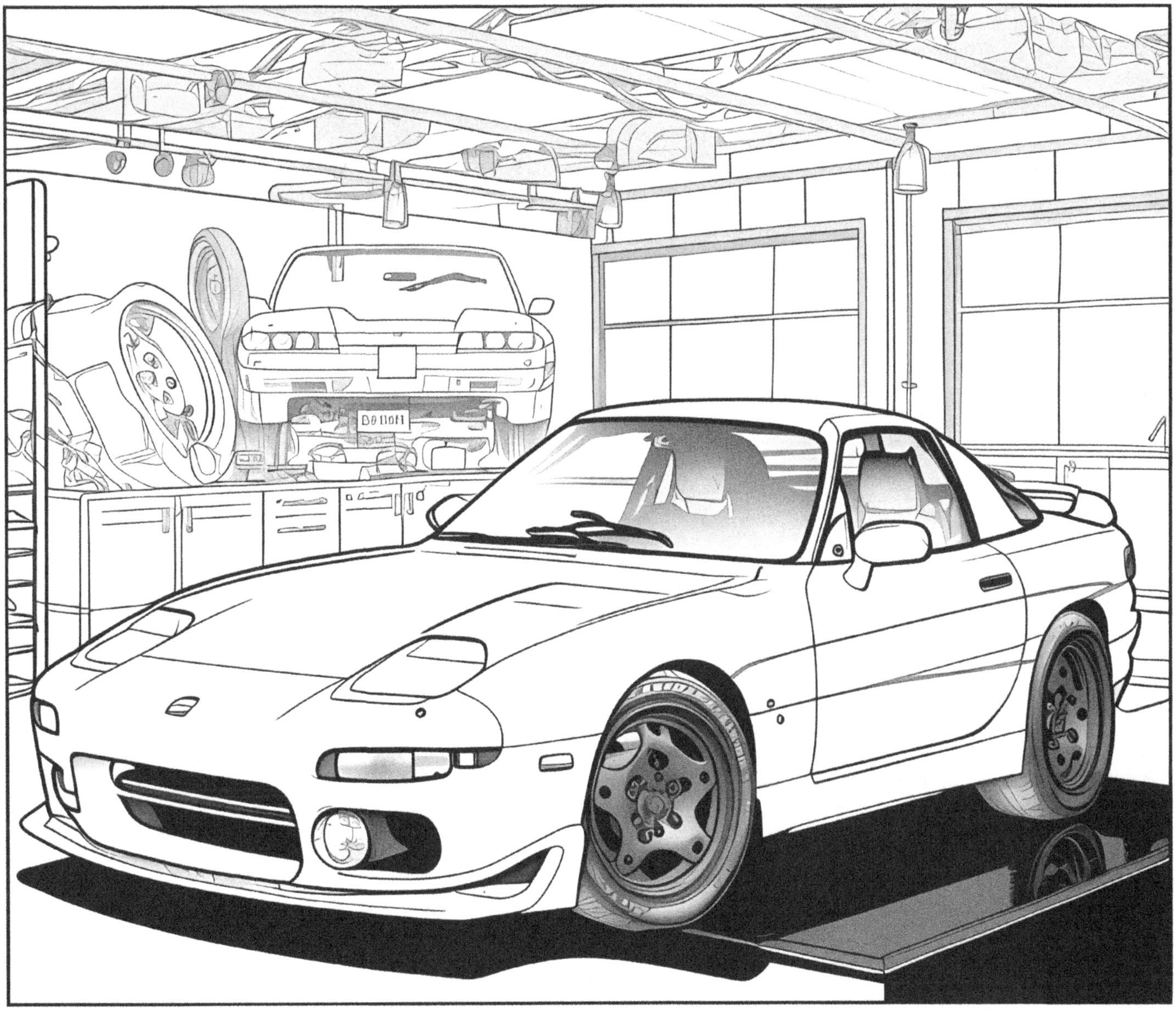

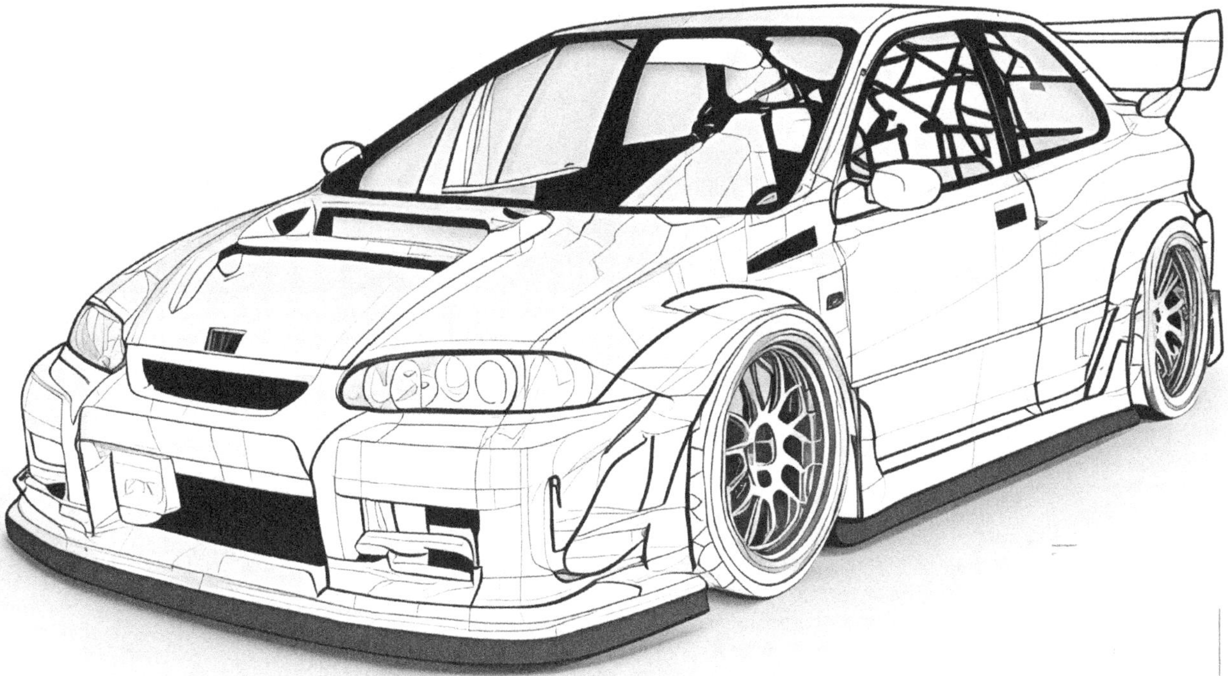

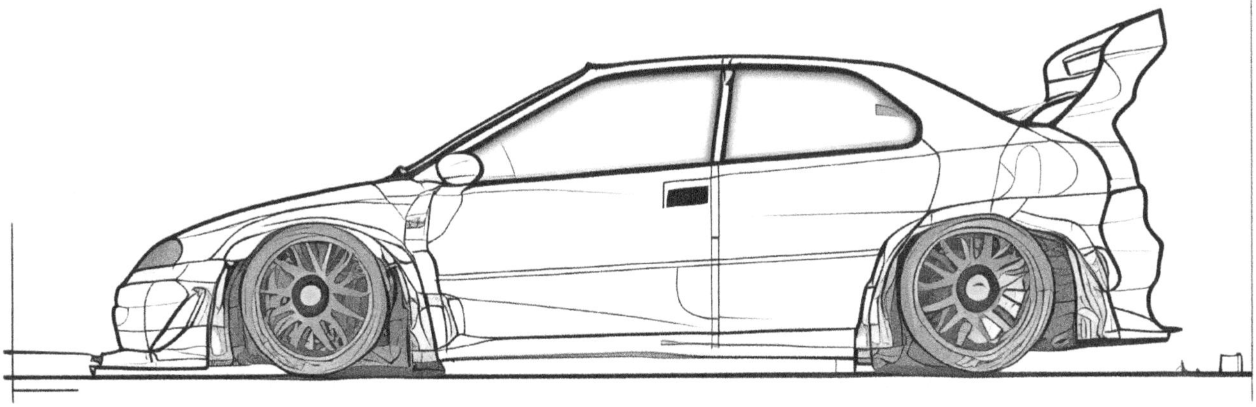

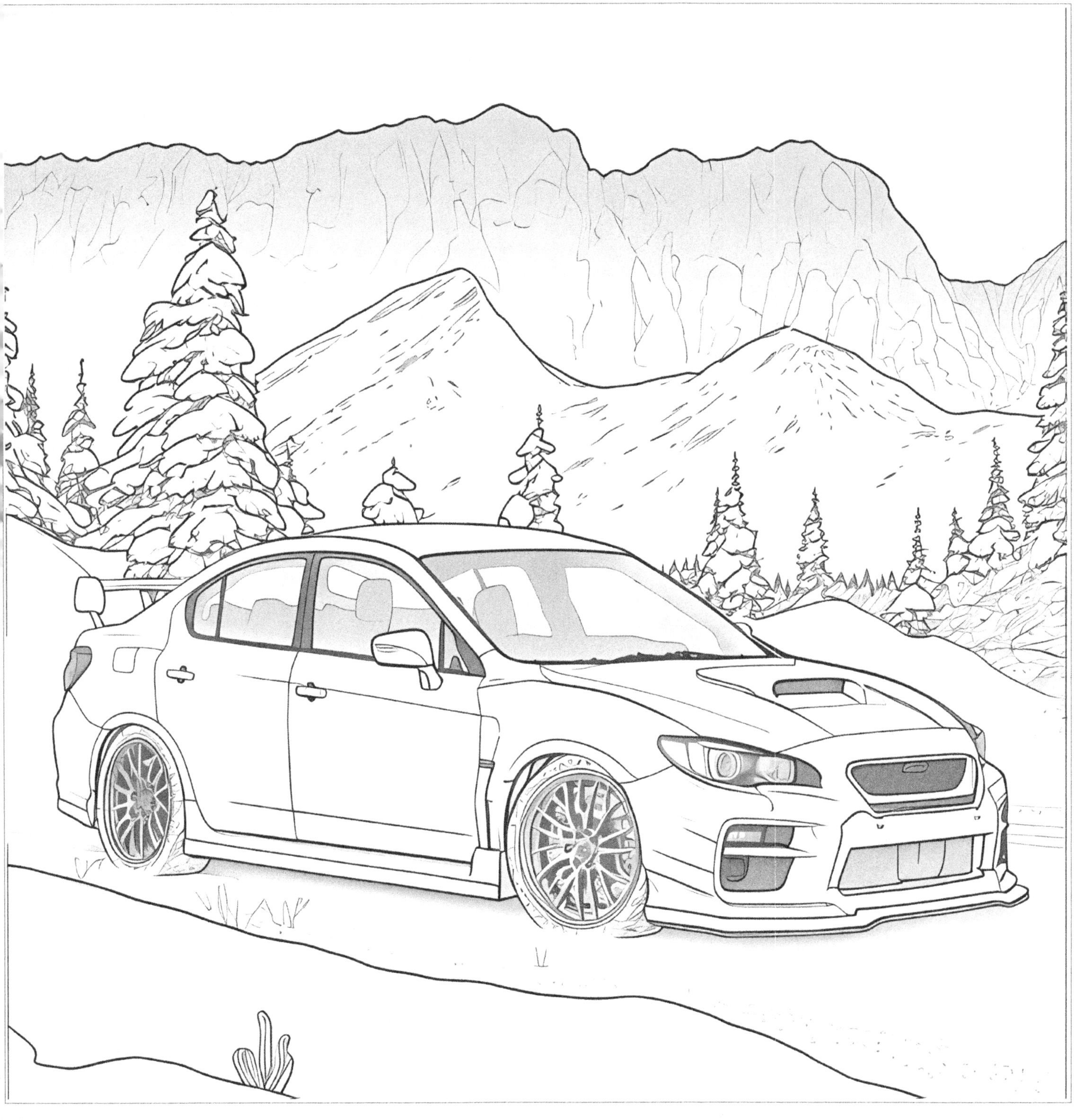

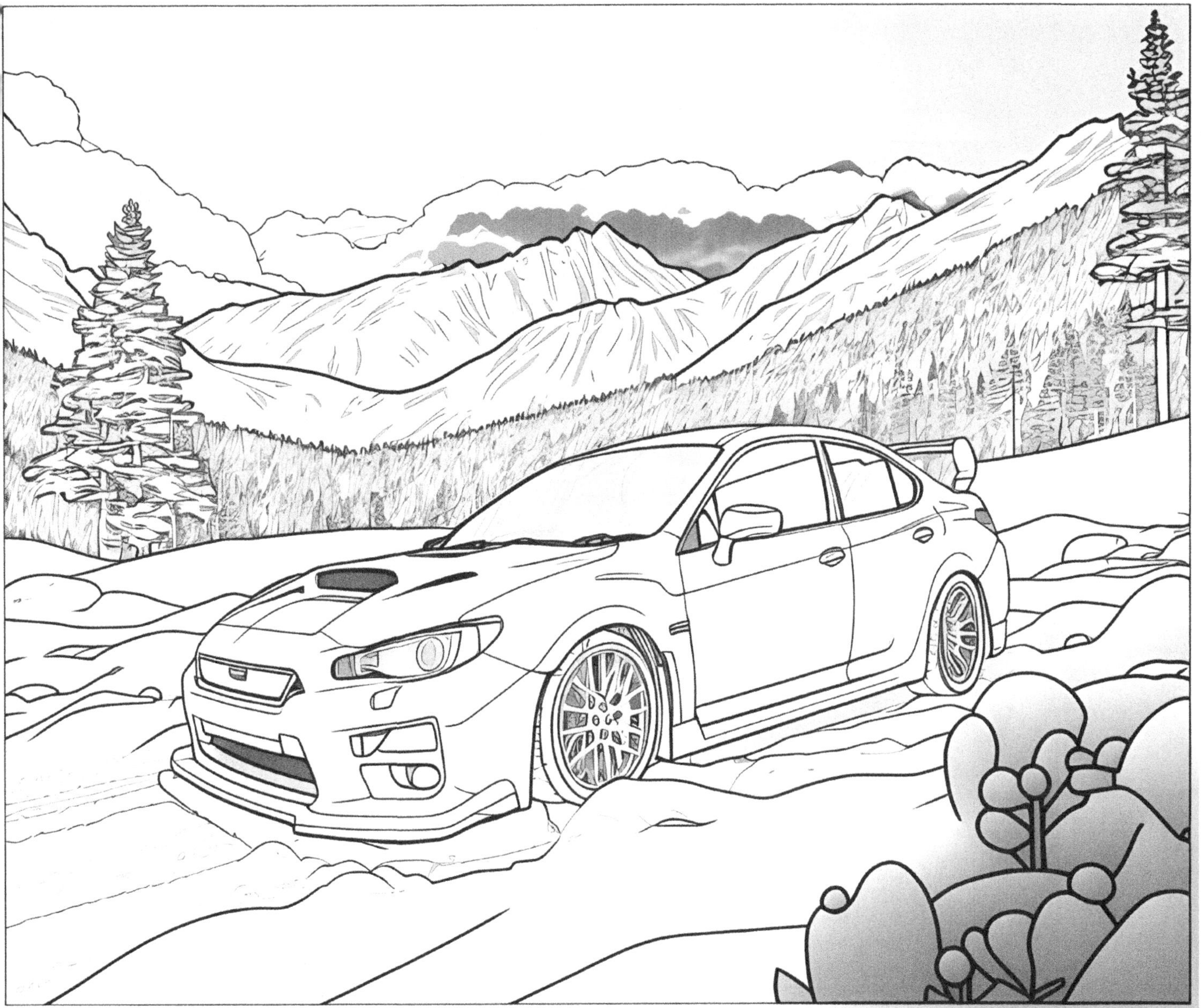

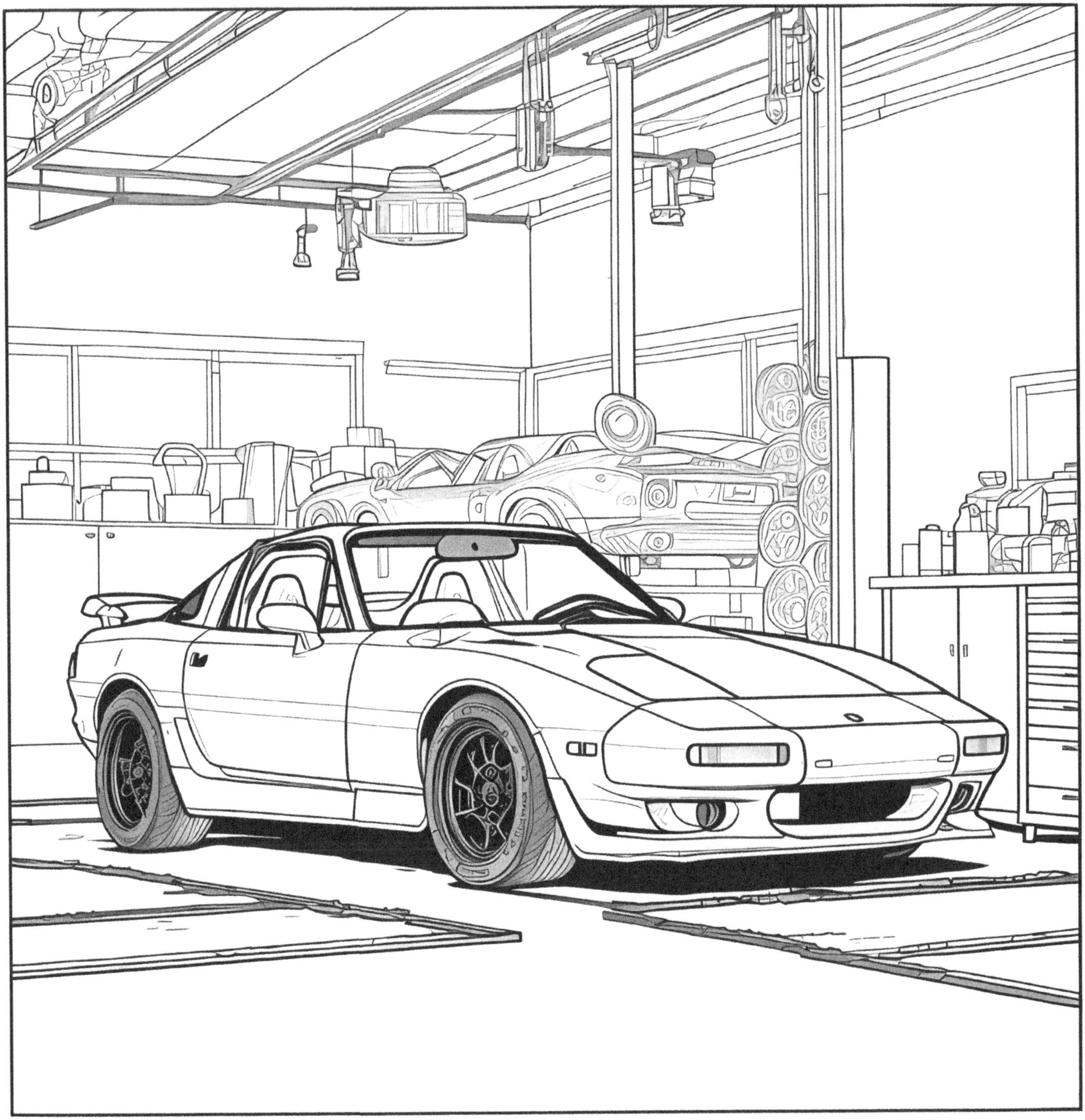

17